Shri Ram Raksha Stotram
Shri Ram Stuti (Marathi)
In English Script

Contributers:

Sage Budhakaushika
Shivali Rakesh Agrawal
Purwa Chakraborty
Publisher: Divinebharat

Shri Ram Raksha Stotram

Shri Ram Stuti (Marathi)

Contributers:

Sage Budhakaushika
Shivali Rakesh Agrawal
Purwa Chakraborty
Publisher: Divinebharat

ISBN: 978-93-5592-782-8
Email: info@divinebharat.com
Website: www.divinebharat.co

Table of Contents

Introduction

The Ram Raksha Stotra is a highly sacred and powerful hymn composed in Sanskrit. According to traditional belief, reciting it grants the divine protection of Shri Ram. The stotra describes the various forms and attributes of Lord Shri Ram, which is believed to free the devotee from difficulties and grant peace, courage, and positive energy. It stabilizes the mind and increases confidence, making its daily recitation extremely beneficial.

Origin of the Ram Raksha Stotra (Traditional Story)

According to tradition, the author of the Ram Raksha Stotra is the Sage Budhakaushika. While he was engaged in intense penance, Lord Shiva appeared to him in a dream one day. Mahadev told him:

"O Budhakaushika! For the welfare of all beings, I am giving you a miraculous stotra. Whoever chants this Ram Raksha Stotra will remain protected from all dangers and will always receive the grace of Shri Ram."

Saying this, Lord Shiva recited the entire stotra to him in the dream. When the sage awoke, he wrote it down exactly as he had heard it. Hence, this hymn is known as "Budhakaushika Krit Ram Raksha Stotra."

Importance of the Stotra

- The stotra is considered the divine armor(kavach) of Lord Shri Ram.
- It is believed to protect the body, mind, home, and family.
- Fear, illness, negativity, and obstacles are removed.

- It brings peace, stability, and courage to the mind.
- It is considered highly auspicious for children, students, and devotees of all ages.

Tradition of Recitation

In many households, it is a daily tradition to recite the Ram Raksha Stotra either in the morning or at night. In Maharashtra, children are even taught this stotra in school.

Ram Stuti: Introduction

Ram Stuti is a beautiful hymn describing the virtues, form, and divine glory of Lord Shri Ram. It awakens devotion in the heart and purifies, calms, and elevates the mind. In Marathi tradition, this stuti is deeply loved.

The hymn portrays Shri Ram's compassionate, righteous, and

courageous nature in very graceful words. Every line reminds the devotee of Shri Ram's grace and offers guidance based on His ideal life.

Benefits of Reciting Ram Stuti

- Removes sorrow, anxiety, and restlessness from the mind.
- Brings harmony, peace, and positivity to the home.
- Increases confidence, courage, and positive energy.
- According to tradition, Shri Ram's grace removes obstacles from one's path.

Tradition of Recitation

Many devotees recite Ram Stuti during Ram Navami, Ramayana readings, and daily worship. Chanting it in a calm atmosphere—morning or evening—brings deep peace and devotion.

|| Om Shriganeshaya Namah ||

Asya Shri Ram Raksha Stotra
Mantrasya
Budhkaushik Rishih
Shri Sita Ram Chandro Devata
Anushtup Chhandah
Sita Shaktih
Shrimad Hanuman Keelakam
Shri Ramchandra Preetyarthe
Ram Raksha Stotra Jape
Viniyogah ||

|| Ath Dhyanam ||

Dhyayed Ajanubahum
Dhrit Shar Dhanusham
Baddh Padmasanastham
Peetam Vaso Vasanam
Nava Kamal Dal Sparadhi
Netram Prasannam ||

Vamangka Aarodh Sita Mukha
Kamala Milal Lochanam
Neeradabham
Nana Alankara Deeptam
Dadhat Uru Jata Mandanam
Ramchandram ||

Iti Dhyanam ||

Shri Ram Raksha Stotram

1
Charitam Raghunathasya
Shatakoti Pravistaram
Ekaikam Aksharam Pumsam
Mahapataka Nashanam
2
Dhyatva Neelotpala Shyamam
Ramam Rajivalochanam
Janaki Lakshmanopetam
Jata Mukuta Manditam

3

Sasi Toon Dhanur Bana
Panim Naktam Charantakam
Svalilaya Jagat Tratum
Avirbhutam Ajam Vibhum

4

Rama Raksham Pathet Prajnah
Papaghneem Sarva Kamadam
Shiro Me Raghavah Patu
Bhalam Dasharathatmajah

5

Kausalyeyo Drishau Patu
Vishwamitra Priyah Shruti
Ghranam Patu Yajna Trata
Mukham Saumitrivatsalah

6

Jihvam Vidya Nidhih Patu
Kantham Bharata Vanditah
Skandhau Divyayudhah Patu
Bhujau Bhagneshakarmukah

7
Karau Sitapatih Patu
Hridayam Jamadagnyajit
Madhyam Patu Khara Dhvamsi
Nabhim Jambavan Ashrayah
8
Sugriveshah Kati Patu
Sakthini Hanumat Prabhuh
Uru Raghuttamah Patu
Rakshahkula Vinashakrit
9
Januni Setukrit Patu
Janghe Dashamukhantakah
Padau Bibhishana Shridah
Patu Ramo Akhilam Vapuh
10
Etam Ramabalopetam
Raksham Yah Sukriti Pathet
Sa Chirayuh Sukhi Putri
Vijayi Vinayi Bhavet

11
Patalabhutala Vyoma
Charinash Chhadmacharinah
Na Drashtum Api Shaktaste
Rakshitam Ramanamabhih
12
Rameti Ramabhadreti
Ramachandreti Va Smaran
Naro Na Lipyate Papaih
Bhuktim Muktim Cha Vindati
13
Jagajjaitreka Mantreṇa
Ramanamnabhirakshitam
Yah Kanthe Dharayettasya
Karasthah Sarvasiddhayah
14
Vajra Panjara Namedam
Yo Ramakavacham Smaret
Avyahatajnah Sarvatra
Labhate Jayamangal

15

Adishtavan Yatha Swapne
Ramarakshham Imam Harah
Tatha Likhitavan Pratah
Prabuddho Budhakaushikah

16

Aramah Kalpavriksanam
Viramah Sakalapadam
Abhiramas Trilokanam
Ramah Shrimaan Sa Nah Prabhuh

17

Tarunau Rupasampannau
Sukumaarau Mahabalau
Pundarikavishalakshau
Chira Krishnajinambarau

18

Phala Moola Shinau Dantau
Tapasau Brahmacharinau
Putrau Dasharathasyaitau
Bhratarau Ramlakshmanau

19

Sharanyau Sarva Sattvanam
Shreshthau Sarva Dhanushmatam
Rakshahkula Nihantarau
Trayetam No Raghuttamau

20

Atta Sajja Dhanushavishu
Sprisha Vakshayashu Gana
Nishanga Sanginau

Rakshanaya Mama Ram
Lakshmanau
Agratah Pathi Sadaiva
Gachchatam

21

Sannaddhah Kavachi Khadgi
Chapabana Dharo Yuva
Gachchan Manoratho Asmakam
Ramah Patu Sa Lakshmanah

22
Ramo Dasharathih Shuro
Lakshmananucharo Bali
Kakutsthah Purushah Purnah
Kausalyeyo Raghuttamah
23
Vedanta Vedyah Yajneshah
Purana Purushottamah
Janaki Vallabhah Shrimaan
Aprameya Parakramah
24
Ityetani Japannityam
Madbhaktah Shraddhayanvitah
Ashwamedhadhikam Punyam
Samprapnoti Na Samshayah
25
Ramam Durva Dal Shyamam
Padmaksam Pita Vasasam
Stuvanti Namabhir Divyaih
Na Te Samsarino Narah

26

Ramam Lakshmana Purvakam
Raghuvaram Sitapatim Sundaram
Kakutstham Karunarnavam
Gunanidhim Viprapriyam
Dharmikam

Rajendram Satya Sandham
Dasharatha Tanayam
Shyamalam Shantamurtim
Vande Lokabhiramam
Raghukul Tilakam
Raghavam Ravanarim

27

Ramaya Ramabhadraya
Ramachandraya Vedhase
Raghunathaya Nathaya
Sitayah Pataye Namah

28

Shri Ram Ram
Raghunandan Ram Ram
Shri Ram Ram
Bharatagendra Ram Ram
Shri Ram Ram
Rankaarkasha Ram Ram
Shri Ram Ram Sharanam
Bhava Ram Ram

29

ShriRamachandra Charanau
Manasa Smarami
ShriRamachandra Charanau
Vachasa Grinami
ShriRamachandra Charanau
Shirasaa Namaami
ShriRamachandra Charanau
Sharanam Prapadye

30

Mata Ramo Matpita
Ramachandrah
Swami Ramo Matsakha
Ramachandrah
Sarvasvam Me
Ramachandro Dayalurnanyam
Jane Naiva Jane Na Jane

31

Dakshine Lakshmano Yasya
Vame Tu Janakatmaja
Purato Marutiryasya
Tam Vande Raghunandanam

32

Lokabhiramam Ranaranga
Dheeram
Rajiva Netram
Raghuvanshanatham

Karunya Rupam
Karunakaram Tam
Shri Ramachandram
Sharanam Prapadye
33
Manojavam Marutatulya
Vegam
Jitendriyam Buddhimattaam
Varishtham
Vatatmajam Vanarayutha
Mukhyam
Shri Ramadutam Sharanam
Prapadye
34
Koojantam Ram Rameti
Madhuram
Madhuraksharam
Aarukhya Kavita Shakham
Vande Valmiki Kokilam

35
Apadam Apahartaram
Dataram Sarvasampadam
Lokabhiramam Shri Ramam
Bhuyo Bhuyo Namamyaham

36
Bharjanam Bhavabeejanam
Arjanam
Sukha Sampadam
Tarjanam Yamadutanam
Ram Rameti Garjanam

37
Ramo Rajamani Sada
Vijayate
Ramam Ramesham Bhaje
Ramena Abhihata
Nishachara Chamu
Ramaya Tasmai Namah

38

Raman Nasti Parayanam
Parataram
Ramasya Daso Asmyaham
Rame Chittalaya Sada Bhavatu
Me Bho Rama Mamuddhara

39

Ram Rameti Rameti
Rame Rame Manorame
Sahasranama Tattulyam
Ramanama Varanane

|| Shri Sita Ramachandra
Arpanam Astu ||

Shri Ramstuti

॥Shri Ram Stuti ॥

Sansar sangebahu shinalo mi ।
Kripa kari re Raghurajaswami ।
Prarabdha maze sahasa talena ।
Tujavin Rama maj kanthavena ॥1 ॥

Man he vikari sthirata na ye re ।
Tyache ni sangebhramate bhale re ।
Apoorva karya man he vitena ।
Tujavin Rama maj kanthavena ॥2 ॥

Mayaprapanchi bahu guntalo re ।
Vishal vyadhimadhe bandhalo re ।
Dehabhimaneati rahavena ।
Tujavin Rama maj kanthavena ॥3 ॥

Daridryadukhe bahu kashtalo mi ।
Sansarmayetachi guntalo mi ।

Sanchit mazemajala kalena ।
Tujavin Rama maj kanthavena ॥4 ॥

Lakshmivilasi bahu saukhya vate ।
ShriRam dhyatam mani kashta mothe

Prapanchavarta vadata vitena ।
Tujavin Rama maj kanthavena ॥5 ॥

Ahoratra dhanda karita purena ।
Prarabdha yogemaj rahavena ।
Bhavadukh mazekadhihi talena ।
Tujavin Rama maj kanthavena ॥6 ॥

Tirthasi jata bahu dukh vate ।
Vishayantari rahuni saukhya vate ।
Swahit mazemajala kalena ।
Tujavin Rama maj kanthavena ॥7 ॥

Mi kothuni kon alo kasa ho ।
Striputra swapnatichi guntalo ho ।

Aise kaloni man he vitena ।
Tujavin Rama maj kanthavena ॥ 8 ॥

Asatya vakyanni mukach jhalo ।
Adattadoshen dukhi budalo ।
Apoorva karani kashi aathavena ।
Tujavin Rama maj kanthavena ॥ 9 ॥

Abrahmamurti bhaj Ramasindhu ।
Chaitanyaswami nija dinabandhu ।
Abhyantari prem mani thasena ।
Tujavin Rama maj kanthavena ॥ 10 ॥

Vishranti dehin anumatra nahi ।
Kulabhimane padalo pravahi ।
Ashantuni door kadhi kalena ।
Tujavin Rama maj kanthavena ॥ 11 ॥

Vishayi jananni maj aalavile ।
Prapanchapashantachi budavile ।
Swahit maze majala disena ।
Tujavin Rama maj kanthavena ॥ 12 ॥

Nardehadoshanvarnu kitire ।
Uchar mazemani vatati re ।
Lalataresha kadhi palatena ।
Tujavin Rama maj kanthavena ॥ 13 ॥

Majala anath prabhu tunch data ।
Mi mudha ki jan asechi ata ।
Dasa manin aathava Virsena ।
Tujavin Rama maj kanthavena ॥ 14 ॥

Printed at Repro India Ltd.